Artists Through the Ages

Édouard Manet

Alix Wood

WINDMILL
BOOKS

New York

Published in 2016 by **Windmill Books**, An Imprint of Rosen Publishing
29 East 21st Street, New York, NY 10010

Copyright © 2016 Alix Wood Books

Adaptations to North American edition © 2016 Windmill Books,
An Imprint of Rosen Publishing

Editor for Alix Wood Books: Eloise Macgregor
Designer: Alix Wood

Photo Credits: Cover, 1 © Steven A. Cohen collection; 4 bottom © Mbzt;
5, 21 © The Walters Art Museum; 6 © Norton Simon Museum; 7, 11 ©
Metropolitan Museum of Art; 8 © Shelburne Museum; 9 © Ny Carlsberg
Glyptotek; 10, 14, 15, 17 © Musée d'Orsay; 12-13 © National Gallery;
16 © Neue Pinakothek; 18-19 © Courtauld Institute of Art; 22-23 ©
nga/Mrs. Horace Havemeyer; 24 © Museo del Prado, Madrid; 25 ©
Kunsthalle Mannheim; 26 © nga; 27 © Alte Nationalgalerie/ Mrs. Félicie
Bernstein; 28 © National Gallery of Victoria; 28 © Dollar Photo Club

Cataloging-in-Publication Data
Wood, Alix.
Édouard Manet / by Alix Wood.
p. cm. — (Artists through the ages)
Includes index.
ISBN 978-1-4777-5592-1 (pbk.)
ISBN 978-1-4777-5593-8 (6 pack)
ISBN 978-1-4777-5444-3 (library binding)
1. Manet, Édouard, — 1832-1883 — Juvenile literature.
2. Painters — France — Biography — Juvenile literature.
I. Wood, Alix. II. Title.
ND553.M3 W66 2016
759.4—d23

Manufactured in the United States of America
CPSIA Compliance Information: Batch #WS15WM:
For Further Information contact Windmill Books, New York, New York at 1-866-478-0556

Contents

Who Was Manet?..............................4

A Son and Then a Wife 6

Traveling and Learning 8

Success at the Salon 10

People Having Fun 12

Unpopular Art 14

Friends and Influences 16

Impressionist? 18

Paris Bars and Cafés......................20

At the Opera..................................22

Painting War 24

Nature and Industry 26

Manet's Last Years 28

Glossary..30

Websites..31

Read More and Index....................32

Who Was Manet?

Édouard Manet was born in 1832 in Paris, France. His family was wealthy. His father was a judge and his mother was the daughter of a **diplomat**. They wanted Manet to become a lawyer, but Manet loved to draw and paint.

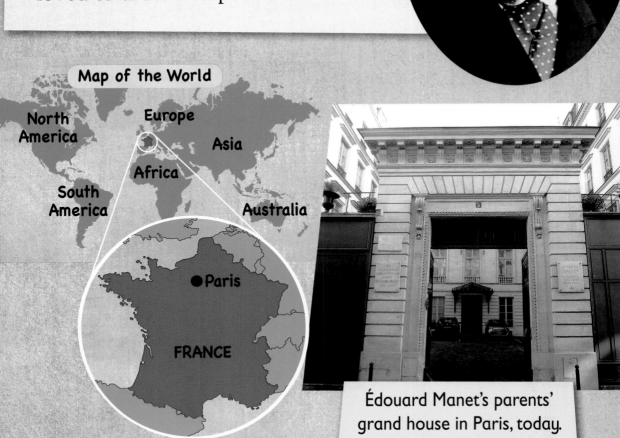

Map of the World

North America

Europe

Asia

Africa

South America

Australia

●Paris

FRANCE

Édouard Manet's parents' grand house in Paris, today.

Manet's father tried to encourage his son to find another profession. He hoped Manet might like to join the navy. At age 16, Manet boarded a navy ship and sailed to Brazil. When Manet returned six months later he failed his naval examinations. He failed them several times and after ten years his parents finally gave in, and supported his dream of attending art school!

Encouragement

Manet's Uncle Edmond was interested in art and encouraged him to paint. He took Manet on trips to the Louvre Gallery to see other painters' work. He encouraged Manet to enroll in a drawing course taught by Thomas Couture. At the class Manet met Antonin Proust, who became a lifelong friend.

Daydreams by Manet's teacher, Thomas Couture

A Son and Then a Wife

Manet fell in love with his young Dutch piano teacher, Suzanne Leenhoff. They had a son, Leon. They did not marry until 11 years after Leon was born. Manet often painted his son, but he introduced him to people as Suzanne's younger brother!

Madame Manet, 1866

Mrs. Manet

Suzanne Leenhoff had been hired by Manet's father to teach his two sons piano. Manet kept their relationship secret. They did not marry until after his father's death.

Boy Carrying a Sword,
1861. The model
is believed to be
Manet's son, Leon.

Traveling and Learning

From 1853 to 1856, Manet visited Germany, Italy, and the Netherlands. He visited galleries and studied painters such as the Dutch painter Frans Hals, and the Spanish artists Diego Velázquez and Francisco de Goya. He visited Venice, Italy, once more with his wife in 1874.

The Grand Canal of Venice (Blue Venice), 1875

When Manet returned from his travels he opened a studio. He started developing a new style of painting. He still used the dark colors of his teacher, Couture, but he no longer layered his paint. He also preferred to paint outdoors.

Real Life

Realism is an art style where artists paint things as they are. They often choose everyday subjects. The man in Manet's *The Absinthe Drinker* was a local Parisian who made a living rummaging through garbage. Manet added the glass of absinthe later.

The Absinthe Drinker, 1859

Success at the Salon

The Salon, Paris, held Europe's most famous art exhibition. It was very difficult to get a work to be selected by the committee. In 1861, Manet had two canvases accepted!

One of the paintings was a portrait of his parents. Manet's father was ill at the time of the portrait and died the following year.

As Manet's father was not happy that he became an artist, perhaps this success at the Salon helped him be proud of his son. The painting wasn't well-liked by the **critics**, though.

Portrait of Mr. and Mrs. Auguste Manet, 1860

The Spanish Singer

Manet's other work, *The Spanish Singer*, was popular. Do you think the model can really play the guitar? He is holding it the wrong way!

People Having Fun

Manet's *Music in the Tuileries* was his first major painting of people enjoying their **leisure** time. It was a new idea to paint this kind of subject. Manet painted himself and some of his friends and family in the picture. Manet is the man looking at us, at the front, second on the left.

Painting Like a Photograph

Some of this painting is detailed, and some is not. The children in the **foreground** are blurred, as if they were moving when a photograph was taken.

Unpopular Art

Manet painted two works that certainly got the art world talking about him. *Olympia* and *Luncheon on the Grass* both featured women with no clothes on. This was not unusual in art, but critics did not like Manet's work at all!

Olympia

Manet's *Olympia* was accepted by the Paris Salon in 1865, where it created a **scandal**. Manet's friend, Proust, said that only the quick action of the exhibition organizers kept the painting from being punctured and torn by the people who came to see it! People did not like the way the model was looking out of the picture at them.

a detail from *Olympia*, 1863

The model in both paintings was Victorine Meurent, who later became a painter herself.

The Balcony, 1868, was exhibited in 1879 at the Salon. Critics did not like the piece. One suggested "Close the shutters!"

Friends and Influences

Manet became friends with the **Impressionist** painters Edgar Degas, Claude Monet, Pierre-Auguste Renoir, Alfred Sisley, Paul Cézanne, and Camille Pissarro. His artist friend Berthe Morisot, who was a member of their group, introduced him to them. Manet was influenced by their Impressionist style, and painted the picture below of Claude Monet in a very loose, light Impressionist style.

Claude Monet in Argenteuil, 1874

Repose –
Berthe Morisot,
about 1870

Berthe Morisot

A successful artist, Morisot persuaded Manet to paint in the open air. Manet used some of her **techniques** in his paintings. In 1874, she married Manet's brother, Eugene.

Impressionist?

Manet did not think of himself as an Impressionist. He liked to exhibit his work at the Salon rather than hold exhibitions with the other Impressionists. However, when Manet's work was rejected from the 1867 Salon, he set up his own exhibition and met many other Impressionists because of it.

His work influenced other Impressionists. He, in turn, was influenced by them, especially Monet and Morisot. Their influence is seen in Manet's use of lighter colors. Manet still used his distinctive black paint, which was not used much by other Impressionists. He painted many outdoor pieces, but always returned to the **studio** to complete what he thought of as his more serious work.

A Bar at the Folies-Bergère, 1882

Paris Bars and Cafés

Manet would visit cafés and bars to **sketch** the people there. In his paintings you get a feel for what ordinary life in Paris was like at the time. People talk, listen to music, drink, read, and wait. Cafés were a common meeting place for Paris artists where they would talk and exchange ideas. Many Impressionists painted scenes in cafés and bars.

The Café Concert, 1878

In this painting (right), the three main figures in the crowded café don't look at each other. The man is watching the performance. You can see the singer reflected in the mirror in the background of the painting. The painting was finished in Manet's studio. Do you recognize the marble countertop? It is the same one that Manet used in his painting on page 19.

At the Opera

Manet painted wealthy people enjoying themselves, too. In *Masked Ball at the Opera*, Manet paints men with top hats and women in masks and costumes enjoying the opera. He put portraits of himself and his friends in the picture. Manet is the man looking straight at us, on the right.

Half-figures

Manet often painted figures that were **cropped** in half at the edges of his paintings. This makes the viewer aware that we are only seeing part of a scene. In this painting there is a pair of legs dangling from the balcony! Painting off the edges makes the opera seem so crowded, it can't all fit on the canvas!

Masked Ball at the Opera, 1873

Painting War

Manet painted the reality of modern life, and that reality included war. In 1870, during France's war against Prussia, Manet served in the National Guard. He helped fight to protect Paris during a four-month **siege**. When Paris surrendered, Manet left to join his family in the south of France. On his return to Paris he found his studio damaged. To raise money to fix it he sold many of his paintings to the art dealer, Paul Durand-Ruel.

Inspired by Goya

On Manet's trips to Spain he had admired the work of the artist Francisco Goya. Goya's painting *The Third of May 1808* shows Spanish rebels being executed by French soldiers.

The Execution of Emperor Maximilian, 1868

Manet painted three versions of the *Execution of Emperor Maximilian*. They are among Manet's largest paintings. Their subject is the execution of the Austrian-born Emperor of Mexico. The paintings were not allowed to be shown in France, as the French had helped put the Emperor Maximilian in power.

Nature and Industry

Manet painted both nature and modern life with the same honest truth. Some of Manet's best works were his **still life** paintings, such as the lilacs pictured right. In the 1870s, the railways were a sign of modern times. Manet was equally happy painting this noisy, smoky subject matter, too.

The Railway, 1872. Although called *The Railway*, you can't see a train! You can just see the smoke, and imagine the engine is where the little girl is looking. Critics found this confusing, and did not like the painting.

Do you recognize the model? She is the women in the painting on page 14. This is the last painting Manet did of her.

Still Life, Lilac Bouquet, 1883

Manet's Last Years

Manet was unwell for the last two years of his life. He still painted and produced some of his best work. He would rest on a couch in his studio between painting. In 1882, he finished *A Bar at the Folies-Bergère* (on pages 18-19) which was hung at the Salon.

Manet painted *The House at Rueil* a year before he died. Manet spent his summer holidays for many years at the house.

The House at Rueil, 1882

Manet's friend, the journalist and politician Antonin Proust, convinced the French government to award Manet the National Order of the Legion of Honor in 1881. The Order is the highest decoration in France.

Manet's Death

As Manet became more unwell he had his left foot **amputated** due to infection. He died eleven days later. He was just fifty-one years old. Manet is buried in the Cemetery de Passy in Paris. His art influenced many painters that came after him. During his lifetime critics did not like some of his work, but he is now considered one of the best artists of his generation.

Glossary

absinthe (AB-sinth)
A green alcoholic drink.

amputated
(AM-pyuh-tayt-ed)
Cut off or removed a limb
by surgery.

critics (KRIH-tiks)
People who write their
opinion about something.

cropped (KROPD)
Removed the upper or outer
parts of something.

diplomat (DIP-loh-mat)
A person employed to keep
up relations between the
governments of different
countries.

foreground
(FOR-grownd)
The part of a scene or
picture that is nearest to
and in front of the viewer.

Impressionist
(im-PREH-shuh-nist)
An artist who concentrates
on the impression of a
scene using unmixed
primary colors and
small brushstrokes to
simulate light.

leisure (LEE-zhur)
Time to do whatever one wants.

realism (REE-uh-lih-zim)
Art that shows nature and everyday life as it exists in the world.

scandal (SKAN-dul)
Conduct that people find shocking and bad.

siege (SEEJ)
Blocking off a fort or a city with soldiers so that nothing can get in or out.

sketch (SKECH)
A quick drawing.

still life (STIL LYF)
A picture of objects that are often carefully arranged by the artist.

studio (STOO-dee-oh)
A room or building where an artist works.

techniques (tek-NEEKZ)
Methods of achieving a desired aim.

Websites

For web resources related to the subject of this book, go to: **www.windmillbooks.com/weblinks** and select this book's title.

Read More

Croton, Guy. *Manet* (The Great Artists and Their World).
New York, NY: Newforest Press, 2010.

Mis, Melody S. *Édouard Manet.* (Meet the Artist). New York, NY:
PowerKids Press, 2007.

Zaczek, Iain. *Édouard Manet.* (Great Artists). New York, NY:
Gareth Stevens, 2014.

Index

A
Absinthe Drinker, The
    9

B
Balcony, The 15
Bar at the Folies-Bergère
    18-19, 28
Berthe Morisot 16, 17,
    18
Boy Carrying a Sword 7

C
Café Concert, The 21
Cézanne, Paul 16
*Claude Monet in
    Argenteuil* 16
Couture, Thomas 5, 9

D
Degas, Edgar 16

E
*Execution of Emperor
    Maximilian* 25

G
Goya, Francisco 8, 24
Grand Canal of Venice 8

H
House at Rueil, The 28

L
Leenhoff, Suzanne 6
Legion of Honor 29
Luncheon on the Grass
    14

M
Madame Monet 6
*Masked Ball at the
    Opera* 22-23
Meurent, Victorine 14,
    26
Monet, Claude 16, 18
Music in the Tuileries
    12-13

O
Olympia 14

P
Pissarro, Camille 16
*Portrait of Mr. and Mrs.
    Auguste Manet* 10
Proust, Antonin 5, 14,
    29

R
Railway, The 26
Renoir, Pierre-Auguste
    16
Repose – Berthe Morisot
    17

S
Sisley, Alfred 16
Spanish Singer, The 11
Still Life, Lilac Bouquet
    27